Zimbabwean born artist, ibizo lami, uses multiple mediums to celebrate their personal experiences and identity. Some core themes in their work are motivations for positive mental health and love of good food. ibizo is the founder and organiser for 'Self Care Saturdays', an online event that discusses the nourishment of the mind, body and spirit.

They are a former cohost of She Grrrowls, a feminist arts night in London and a regular feature at the Edinburgh Fringe Festival. ibizo lami has performed live at multiple poetry events across the country including That's What She Said and Spoken Word London.

ibizo has completed a run of *Chosen Family* at Brighton Fringe Festival, which has been adapted here for the page by Burning Eye Books.

Chosen Family

ibizo lami

Burning Eye

BurningEyeBooks
Never Knowingly
Mainstream

This first edition published by Burning Eye Books 2022

www.burningeye.co.uk

@burningeyebooks

Burning Eye Books
15 West Hill, Portishead, BS20 6LG

ISBN 978-1-913958-17-6

CHOSEN
FAMILY

Content note: This collection addresses explicit details of rape, mental disorder and recovery.

For Michelle

*Although we passed through the same womb,
it truly feels like we chose one another.*

CONTENTS

Dr Unicorn

After meeting once a month for the past three years, Dr
Unicorn recommended reading *David and Goliath*. Not
the Bible story, but the book by Malcolm Gladwell. It had a
chapter about those crucial first appearances, about how eyes
and logic can be deceiving.

Goliath's huge growth spurt and illusion of strength were
likely the result of a genetic disease. Although huge and bulky,
Goliath was also a bit blind and very slow: something to do
with the protein synthesis in his body. His heavy armour didn't
help much.

Now, David.

David David David.

Seemingly unthreatening and small, used a slingshot to
herd sheep from a young age, protecting his herd, cracking
the skulls of predators from a distance. An agile, limber
marksman, he intimately knew his weapons, the size and shape
of stones to pick.

I wanted my own narrative to read like that of David. I
became obsessed with finding the positive things in the
negatives. Seemed to me like God favoured David by making
him that way.

What was I uniquely gifted with?

Rewind and play back my life and all the challenging
experiences. I found my strength in real people.

I had been given something better than David.

An opportunity to choose my family.

Disadvantage

I summon the strength
to check my phone again,
expose my fingers to the cold:
bus coming in about twenty minutes.

Look to my right.
Check plastic rectangle blue luggage,
clasp my hands around it – still there
as my body rests on the apricot bench.

Carefully open the white paper bag.
Pick out the napkin,
plastic spoon tinted maroon
and a steaming pot of

nausea.
Swallow a bit.
It's OK, throat.

Suddenly,
think back on the yoga studio.
Before it happened.
No inkling.

Belly rise.
    Belly fall—

THE PILLS ARE KILLING MY
BODY. EYES ARE YELLOW.
JAUNDICE. BODY WANTS TO BE
CARRIED HOME. MARVE, HE.
STOP!

--Belly rise.
    Belly fall.

Can't hide this from Mum.
My eyes definitely are yellow.

Belly rise.
        Belly fall.

Jaundice, the internet said.
Common side effect of some antiretrovirals.
How do I tell my mum?
What if she asks if he used a condom?
Or if he was a stranger?
Would it be a lighter blow?

Belly rise.
        Belly fall.

I'm in Kingston waiting for the 418.
Cold, crisp air.
Clean. Tidy.
Pale grey clouds,
concrete pavements,
councils sweep the streets,
shops entice.
Pale pinks, turquoise, blues,
reds, white skin, teeth glaring.

This feels more like home.
Shame looms over me.
I no longer understand
the land that birthed me.
The mishmash:
vibrant green,
pungent odours,
exhaust pipes,
old vehicles,
bodies smelling ripe,
baking in the sun all day,
the bustling of people,
minibus stations lamalokitshi.

Belly rise.
        Belly fall.

I have opened the lid.
Inside, porridge sprinkled
with seeds and honey.
No spillages or burns.
First mouthful.
Chew slowly.
Swallow.

What stories do I bring
from ekhaya other than:

uMarve had sex with me as I slept.
I was passed out on the same bed as him.
The next morning
I strung his cum out of me,
let my fingers coax it out.
I let the water drag it down the drain.

Belly rise.
          Belly fall.

What if I have to take these pills
for the rest of my life?

Belly rise.
          Belly fall.

Second mouthful.
Chew slowly.
Breathe.
Don't cry.
Tell those tears to stop.
Focus on the cold.
Eat.

Belly rise.
          Belly fall.

You're at the bus stop in Kingston.

Advantage

I tell myself I am beautiful each morning.

Initially it felt numb,
no warning,
separate from me.

My head
space
struck in place.

The rest
remote,
floating close by.

I tell myself I am beautiful each morning.

It didn't feel like anything.
The unknown bellows
from parts strewn around,
levitating,
unrelenting.

I couldn't feel it most often,
just watched as an outsider.
Tried to make sense,
unsuccessful.
Ngingasazazi.
Wandering aimlessly.
Not enjoying here nor there.

I tell myself I am beautiful each morning.

A stranger became my flesh,
squatted in my body.
Had a whale of a time.
Threw a party,

vandalised,
spray painted:
numb
dirty
corrupted
unclean
empty

      I tell myself I am beautiful each morning.

Didn't want to look down.
Forgot about feeling,
forgot,
forgot.

      I tell myself I am beautiful each morning.

Woke up.
Gradually
learning,
sometimes fighting,
slowly
remembering.

This is here. Now. Mine.

      I tell myself I am beautiful each morning.

a battle took place on and within delicate flesh scar tissue
formed stronger than before made whole again having learnt
to feel again having learnt to reconnect when body hurts hurts
so much it turns off feeling

      I tell myself I am beautiful each morning.

Careful compassionate
coaxing sweet somethings:

'GOOD MORNING NOZI :)
TODAY IS GOING TO BE AN AMAZING DAY!
I AM AMAZING, BEAUTIFUL,
INTELLIGENT & PHENOMENAL.'

I tell myself I am beautiful each morning

The stranger vacated.
Returned my flesh,
body in disrepair,
unrecognisable shape,
dull skin,
bitter taste in my mouth,
hair unkempt,
but whole.

I tell myself I am beautiful each morning.

I am at ease on a yoga mat;
deep appreciation sweeps my being.
I feel the vibrancy,
chitter chatter,
humming of life beneath my skin.

I tell myself I am beautiful each morning.

A love that previously did not reside here
radiates from within.
Settles in,
turns on the heating,
lights scented candles,
runs a hot bath,
drops lavender in the water.
Immersing myself in self-care.
A compassion drenched in understanding
sweeps over me.

Happy to have lived long enough to see today so I can
        tell myself I AM BEAUTIFUL each morning.

Back to Dr Unicorn

Don't just sit there, find a distraction!

Plopped into a chair, in the waiting room, I pick up a trashy gossip magazine. Whose fillers have destroyed whose lips? Whose bad boy boyfriend has resorted to his old bad boy ways? No longer preoccupied with nesting and creating a family, rather doing ratchet like they were a year ago before coupling up on a reality show, getting married and starting a family straight after.

The people all have different names, but they all look the same: light brown leather tan glistening sexy toned processed meat with intensely illuminated white teeth—

Remember what they taught you in group therapy, look at something more constructive.

OK, change of scenery: *Home and Gardening*, or *Gardening and Home*. Whichever magazine shows you how to grow plants and trees and landscape any spaces you have. These people are pale compared to the gossip magazine people, but they are not pale pale, cz they spend time outdoors in the British sun.

The gardening magazine is more open-plan writing: lots of calm white backgrounds, lots of comfortable living middle-aged and above. Actually rare to see anyone pictured there who is under forty. Species and variations of flowers and fruits perfectly trimmed, laid out, presented. Finery. Gardens actually behaving. This magazine is for people who can afford to take deep breaths.

My inner voice changes accent and pace in accordance with this rich white way of writing. Like the beginnings of a BBC documentary opening on sweeping images of the countryside. Shots of green hills, fields, views from mountaintops, the lush tranquil and abundance. The referencing of lords, dukes, current and past aristocracy:

This tree was planted by Queen Victoria and its twin is now—

Erm, how can trees have twins?

I catch the eye of a toddler sitting next to me in the waiting room. Without much vocabulary, he signals for me to play a game he has just invented. He raises his little hand up every time he notices me so that I high-five him. This goes on for about twenty minutes, with him giggling every time our hands clap.

They are cute, right? That joy and glee and wonder. That nothing is gonna stop me cashing fun today as I try to eat all the floor! confidence.

Watching him trying to eat the floor. Cute edible cheeks outstretched as he tries to fit the whole ground into his mouth—

'MISS MATH?'

Dr Unicorn is calling me.

To this day he calls me 'Miss Math'. Like how you pronounce Maths. Math. Even though the 'H' in my name is silent. Not once has he attempted to say Nozipho. Not once have I ever corrected him. I mean, I have caught the British, so it is just too embarrassing to mention now. I have become like the people of my adoptive country: being overly polite to the point of unnecessary awkwardness.

Once I saw him as I was coming out of Wilko. He was on the phone. Still maintaining his professionalism. Acknowledged me in a respectful manner and went about his business.

OK, he is the first person who taught me how to be empathetic and still put up boundaries. I mean, Pamela (English Pamela), Sophie and Michelle (Australian Michelle) also taught me this. But Dr Unicorn said, 'You have friends for certain things in life. Some friends you might go playing football with only, there's friends you go to the cinema with, friends who you can talk about certain things with and friends who you can rely on when things go bad.'

He also showed me how to value my time outside work. To defend myself. To nurture my gut instinct. To put me first. To trust in my feelings and act accordingly.

Yep, he defo challenged the people pleaser within me. *Wow, I can say 'no'? And nothing bad will happen?*

Like, no one will hate me?
Even better, I will be respected?
Mind blown! (bomb sound effect)

Maybe this is inappropriate. But I sometimes imagine maybe the lessons Dr Unicorn is teaching me are like the universe giving me a supportive father. I feel like Dr Unicorn actually offers real practical help. I've been lowkey absorbing knowledge from him I think my dad was meant to teach me.

Although I was blessed with two father figures from infancy, a biological father and a stepfather, I am now aware that neither had the skills to nurture my emotional needs. Due to family dynamics and cultural traditions, my stepfather kept away from anything to do with raising me outside financial support. Not wanting to step on my biological mother and father's toes. In situations where I was experiencing an extreme crisis, my stepfather offered trivial advice:

'You will get over it.'

'Don't think too much.'

My biological dad unwillingly and rarely engaged in conversations about my emotional wellbeing. If I disclosed any emotional pain, he would downplay or deny my experience. At worst he would find a way to blame and shame me:

'I had it worse when I was a child.'

'You are lucky you can go to school.'

'Just focus on your grades.'

'Don't embarrass us.'

'What will people say when they hear of this?'

But my parents could not have taught me what they did not know.

Dr Unicorn went above and beyond to understand me and what I was going through emotionally. Although at times he would not fully understand some of the things I relayed, he still found ways to soothe me by recommending books that tackled similar topics.

I appreciate that his recommendations also nurtured the ambitious young black woman within me, like when he recommended Oprah Winfrey's biography. He's cool like that.

Always saying things that are inspiring. Like by going in that office I always come out dreaming bigger.

I head into the office as the child demolishes the floor.

Guurl!

When reading this poem, shout out the 'YiiiYiiYii' parts.

Guurl and I decided this sound
would be our warrior woman greeting
to one another.

YiiiYiiYiiYiiYiiiYiiYiiYiiYiiYiiYiiYii

I am reminded of how a year before we met
our friendship seemed inconceivable.
It was during a psychotherapy session.
I was sat on a chair or a sofa,
maybe in the art room
or the eighties vintage bright room.
Both close to the dining room and kitchen, where the summer
barbecues
celebrating our recovery journeys were held.

As I coiled further into my seat,
I explained to my therapist,

> Most often it feels like I live in a desert.
> It's hard maintaining long friendships for me.
> I am too unusual,
> sometimes it scares people.
> I'm hard to pin down,
> have been told I am mysterious.
> I've heard others complain
> of friends who are complex.
> Maybe it's not nice,
> fitting people into more than one box.
> Sometimes people like the idea of me
> but don't really like having me around too tough.
> Sometimes my 'out there' fun side
> gets confused for destructive behaviour.
> Sometimes my super arty side

is mistaken for pretentiousness.
Sometimes I am not pretentious enough.
Sometimes I feel too much,
I am too sensitive.
It gets lonely.
It is lonely.
Once in a while,
I might make a friend
where I feel there is a deep connection.
Someone who sees me and accepts me for me.
Even if it's just for a short while.
It feels like the rare occasions
when it actually rains in the desert.

YiiiYiiYiiYiiYiiiYiiYiiYiiYiiYiiYiiYiiYii

Guuuurl!
Hey, chika!
Hey, Guurl, hey – what's good, what it is? What's up?
Ppsshhhhhh guuuurl!
Kmt chalé!

YiiiYiiYiiYiiYiiiYiiYiiYiiYiiYiiYiiYiiYii

Board games with her are lit! We are so in sync with each other.

You know that scene in *Four Christmases*
where they play *Taboo*?
That couple that gets all their questions correct?
She referenced that during a game of *Heads Up!*,
realising we were now framing
questions like that.
Not really based on describing the noun,
rather describing our shared experiences with said noun.

YiiiYiiYiiYiiYiiiYiiYiiYiiYiiYiiYiiYiiYii

Thing is she is so much fun to be around!
You know that innocent good fun?

Like meeting up after work for dinner,
going to concerts, sharing tweets,
motivational videos, jokes, references, gossip.
OK, the good type of gossip where you pull up
your popcorn and snacks – you know!

YiiiYiiYiiYiiYiiiYiiYiiYiiYiiYiiYiiYiiYii

Hanging out with her feels like we are characters
in *Angus, Thongs and Perfect Snogging*
or any other celebration of teen girl friendship.
Except we are 'adults' now and we talk about detoxes,
debating the benefits of apple cider vinegar
or holding the urge to poop from 5pm until 9pm.
No time between day job and late meeting
to go home and safely have 'me time'.
That's what we call pooping now: 'me time'.

YiiiYiiYiiYiiYiiiYiiYiiYiiYiiYiiYiiYiiYii

Like, we share so much!
She taught me Freetown in Sierra Leone
wasn't like a typical African city
in terms of culture.
Like they don't have native black African languages,
only Krio.
It was the city the emancipated former slaves –
black people –
moved to after they left America.
She asked me blankly one time,

'Haven't you noticed my surname?'

'I thought it was none of my business, like,
I did question why you have a European-sounding
first and last name
when your family are black African.
I didn't wanna be that person, you know—'
Eye roll!

YiiiYiiYiiYiiYiiiYiiYiiYiiYiiYiiYiiYiiYii

She also taught me how method acting is dangerous.
Like legit dangerous.
Like that moody, broody Michael B Jordan
'Hey, Auntie' character
had actually seeped into his persona.
When it comes to emotions and thoughts,
the mind finds it difficult
to tell whether we are pretending.
With enough repetition,
the mind adopts whatever you feed into it.

YiiiYiiYiiYiiYiiiYiiYiiYiiYiiYiiYiiYiiYii

We pondered why we didn't have close guy friends who are
straight.
Quickly assessed the issue that none of our straight guy
friends ever want to chat or delve deeper into how they are
truly feeling.

'You know, it doesn't have to be deep chats.
Just let me know at great length how you feel about
something.
Even if it's just a new song or a pair of jeans.'

Like, I have yet to have a deep regular conversation
with a straight platonic male friend.
I mean, are we right?
Is it a guy thing?
Do straight guys have deep talks with their guy friends?

YiiiYiiYiiYiiYiiiYiiYiiYiiYiiYiiYiiYiiYii

The 'sleepovers',
real chats that overrun into 5am
only meant to last until 10pm tops
because we have jobs, uni, businesses, side hustles,
beauty sleep and self-care to get back to.

Boi, do we chat!
We leave voice note upon voice note.
Like instant pen palling.

'Good morning!'

'IYAHHH!'

'YiiiYiiYiiYiiYiiiYiiYiiYiiYiiYiiYiiYiiYii!'

She sings her punchlines.
Riffs from hip-hop classics
to the contemporary genre-bending songs.

Videos of her rapping and singing along to J Cole
in the bright sunny early hours of winter
as she makes her way to uni
and I send her a video literally giggling
and in awe of my breakfast I am about to eat.
Sunny-side runny yolk eggs with refried Mexican beans.
Seasoning on point! *Yebo!*

YiiiYiiYiiYiiYiiiYiiYiiYiiYiiYiiYiiYiiYii

The first time I read her energy
I wanted to be her friend.
Her hashtag melanin poppin'!
Black girl magic in Epsom
– *Guurl!* – OK, Surrey.
Rocking that boujee, dreadlock, white sundress,
meditating on the beach, clear blue waters,
little gold beads glistening on her locks
and she sang and wrote poetry.

Did I mention she is a black woman living in Surrey
who also likes spoken word poetry?!
She is multidimensional,
contradictory poles that harmonise;
she could fly to the moon tomorrow
and the world would be in awe.

YiiiYiiYiiYiiYiiiYiiYiiYiiYiiYiiYiiYiiYii
Her kindness is unparalleled.
Never shows up empty-handed.
Our interactions memorialised
by objects that accentuate
her appreciation for me.
From a journal to lemon M&S tarts
to Sierra Leone home-cooked food.
She reaffirms
with her love language of gifts
that all of me is worthy of affection.
To be treated with tenderness.
Especially the parts I consider most weird:
my spontaneous expressions of glee
and goofiness.

YiiiYiiYiiYiiYiiiYiiYiiYiiYiiYiiYiiYiiYii

When the parts of me most riddled
with shame popped up,
Guurl soothed and honoured them.
This allowed me to create
space to recognise, listen to,
learn and detach from
pushing people away,
reenacting fears of abandonment.

YiiiYiiYiiYiiYiiiYiiYiiYiiYiiYiiYiiYiiYii!!

With the help of Guurl,
I am maturing into a secure attachment style.
I feel less like I am living in a desert.
It's like I am living in a rainforest
with high and continuous rainfall.
Plenty of opportunities, species,
plants rich in medicinal properties,
nutrient-dense fruits. Self-sustaining,
perfectly balanced ecosystem
of bountiful respect and
freedom to show all parts of me
whilst embracing others
just the way they are.

Elektra

*This is a celebration of a friend's impeccable style, always
ready for a prestige fashion shoot. For the purposes of this
poem she shall be named Elektra, after the character played
by Dominique Jackson.*

Boooouuuujee!
Bouj bouj bouj
            styling!
styling! styling! styling!
SHE'S GIVING ME LYYYYYYFE, HAAAAAHNEY!

Prestige art writer,
model qualities,
sharp wit,
love for Elektra!

                              Pose!

Boy crushes!

                              Pose!

Advancing in the art field!

                              Pose!

Contemporary African Art Fair *daaarling*,
Barber Shop Chronicles,
cultured-ish on Saturdays.
We speak each other's names, accents and all.

                              Pose!

Sleepovers,
Notting Hill Carnival 2017,
Black Cultural Archives,
Yauatcha restaurant.

                              Pose!

Elektra is very intelligent.
Like, super intelligent.
Like whatever she says qualifies for academic writing.
We bonded over our love for gallery art,
Pose the TV show,
our hate for Jamie AKA Ghost in Power,
that glorified, good-looking wasteman –
we scorn the maltreatment
of a dark-skinned black woman.

Pose!

Elektra regularly drops pearls of knowledge,
most of which have been the subject
of numerous bestsellers,
made plenty of authors wealthy.

Pose!

'It's disgusting,' she says,
'the way black men are seen as walking big penises.
The Karens in training fucking it up again.
Unleashing an insidious form of racism.'

Pose!

'Put on your highest heels;
your clothes are your armour.
Crush the haters!
Especially the ones in the office.
With the clack of your heels,
they will know to be afraid
before you even enter the room.'

Pose!

I want to say Elektra has sharp edges,
but they are perceived and not really there.

Only serving sharp precise edges in her clothing,
tailored to a T!
Mind you, she is sharp!
Her wit cuts through glass.
Better watch out if you intend
on insulting her or the people she cares for.

Pose!

Next year,
we will wrap ourselves
in contemporary art
at the Dakar Biennale.
We will continue treating ourselves like the deities we are.

Pose!

Grounded in who we are,
our souls, housed within black skin.
Honouring ourselves.
Taking up all the space.
Walking,
seeing,
exploring
this earth.
Our birthright.

Epilogue

'Miss Math?'

He signals for me to start speaking. Draws his chair closer and looks me in the eyes. He is the only man in my life to have done so.

I know he is a general practitioner and I am his client, but there is a sense of him caring, rooting for me to be the best that I can in this life. From his affirmations to his body language. He sees my pain, laughter, joy, hard work and resilience. He sees my humanness and appreciates me for who I am.

I would love to say this is a dynamic he shares with me only, but Dr Unicorn is also the GP for my stepdad, mum and sister. They all feel the same way about him. My stepdad jokes regularly, saying, 'Lowu ulungekakhulu 'ngan'kuthwa uwonile.'

('Dr Unicorn is so lovely and good,
it's almost as if it's an act to cover up
something bad he has done.')
This is a very high compliment in Zimbabwe
(our humour is different, lol).

Chewing Dr Unicorn's ear off, sometimes guiding him haphazardly through the events of the last month, it is easy to forget the purpose of our appointments.

Always, he is fascinated to hear my stories. Shares a book, article or podcast. He recommended Desert Island Discs when I first started seeing him. I was working in insurance at the time, and the latest person to have been interviewed that week on the show was Inga Beale, who was the new CEO of Lloyd's of London. The first woman to hold the position of CEO within the whole insurance industry. As if that isn't a huge accomplishment in itself, she is also queer!

Dr Unicorn provided role models for me. I don't know if it was planned, but Dr Unicorn provided an endless stream of role models, of those who walk on the road less travelled.

Without Dr Unicorn, I don't think I would have had
the awareness to truly maintain the beautiful, nurturing
relationships I have with Guurl and Elektra. My chosen family
is proof to me that families come in all shapes and sizes,
outside gender norms, with or without children. They helped
me discover the necessity of having people who you can
practice unconditional love with. People thrive and open
up to manifest their truest selves when engaged in healthy
close connections with others. A book recommendation
from Dr Unicorn led me down a path to where I tell myself
I am beautiful each morning. Guurl's kindness provided the
safe space I needed to confront past hurts and embrace my
vivacious self. Elektra's celebration of black womanhood gave
me the strength to take up even more space.

The bonds I have with Dr Unicorn, Guurl and Elektra
helped me slay the Goliaths in my life. Like David, I was given
situations that at face value seemed dire, but those moments
revealed the beauty, power and immeasurable rewards of
choosing my own family.

ACKNOWLEDGEMENTS

Thank you to my chosen family who have brought colour into my life. Thank you to my parents, siblings and relatives who despite the dynamics we were born into, still brought so much joy into my life.

Thank you to my editor Bridget Hart who offered me so much support and believed in me. Also thank you to Paul Forster for introducing me to Bridget. Thank you to the rest of the Burning Eye team, Clive Birnie and Harriet Evans.

Thank you to Carmina Masoliver who encouraged me to submit my manuscript to Burning Eye Books.

Thank you to all the mental health professionals who have supported me throughout my recovery journey.

Thank you to everyone who has shown me kindness and given me the space to manifest my truest self.